Everyday Health

INSURANCE BASICS

Globe
Fearon

Parsippany, New Jersey
www.pearsonlearning.com

Reviewers

Sheila Nigh
Wichita Public Schools, Wichita KS 67203

Lois Lanyard
Woodbridge High School, Woodbridge NJ 07095

Linda Jacobs, Ed.D.
The Harbour School, Annapolis MD 21401

Marilyn Pobiner
Black Mountain Middle School, San Diego CA 92129

Linda Stibick
Human Resources, Simon and Schuster, Old Tappan NJ 07675

Credits

Project Editors	Douglas Falk, Stephanie Cahill, Jennifer McCarthy
Executive Editor	Joan Carrafiello
Market Manager	Margaret Rakus
Assistant Market Manager	Donna Frasco
Editorial Development	WordWise, Inc.
Production Editor	John Roberts
Production Director	Kurt Scherwatzky
Interior Design	Pat Smythe
Illustrator	Steven Cavallo
Electronic Page Production	Lesiak/Crampton Design
Cover Design	Pat Smythe
Cover Art	James McDaniel
Editorial Assistant	Eugene Myers

Printed in the United States of America
4 5 6 7 8 9 10   05 04 03 02 01

ISBN 0-8359-3376-8

TABLE OF CONTENTS

TO THE STUDENT

Welcome to *Everyday Health!* By using this series of books, you will achieve these goals:

- You will be able to set goals and make decisions about your health.

- You will be able to help your family and your community in health matters.

- You will be able to practice behavior to improve health.

- You will be able to reduce risks to your health.

- You will understand your role in preventing disease.

- You will understand how to use health information about products.

- You will be able to communicate with others about improving health.

EVERYDAY HEALTH
INSURANCE BASICS

This book will help you understand what health insurance is all about.

Do you know why health insurance is important to you? How does insurance help you meet the high cost of health care today? Lessons in this book have the information to answer these questions.

When you have finished this book, you will know why people need health insurance today. You will be able to make decisions about what kind of health insurance meets your needs. You'll also know how to apply for health insurance, how much it costs to buy, and how to use insurance to pay for your health care.

What Is Health Insurance?

Health care costs a lot of money today. How do families pay for doctor and hospital bills? People buy health insurance to help pay for their health care.

Lesson Objectives

You will be able to

- explain why it is important to have health insurance.
- identify typical services covered by health insurance.

Words to Know

affordable	low enough in cost to pay for without difficulty
insurance	protection you buy from a company to help you pay the costs of health care or damage from fire or accidents
health insurance	kind of insurance that pays for part of your medical expenses and health care
injury	harm or damage to a person
coverage	types of health care that insurance will pay for

Robert found his mother sitting in the kitchen. She was looking at papers that were scattered all over the table.

"Hi Mom," said Robert. "What are you doing?"

"I'm looking over your father's medical bills," answered Robert's mother. "We finally have all the bills from your dad's operation last month."

"That looks complicated," said Robert.

"It is," said his mother.

"Did Dad's operation cost a lot of money?" asked Robert.

"Yes, it was very expensive," answered his mother. "It's a good thing we have health insurance. If we didn't, I'm not sure how we would ever pay these bills."

"How much did the operation cost?" Robert asked.

"I don't know for sure yet," answered Robert's mother. "But look here. The hospital room alone cost $600 for one day. Your father was in the hospital for 10 days."

"Wow!" exclaimed Robert. "That's $6,000 just for the hospital room. What about all the doctors and all the medicine?"

"Sit down," said Robert's mother. "Let's look through these bills and see if we can answer your questions."

The High Cost of Health Care

Robert's father was sick for several months. He visited the doctor many times before he knew what was wrong. He had a serious problem with his heart. He needed an operation to fix his heart condition.

Robert and his mother added up all of his father's doctor and hospital bills. Robert was shocked—so was his mother. The amount was $300,000. How would Robert's family ever pay all the bills?

Most people do not make enough money to support a family and pay huge medical bills. Robert's father is a high school teacher. He is lucky. He will have help paying for his operation.

What would your family do if someone was very sick and had to go into a hospital? How would your family pay for the hospital room? How would they pay for all the doctor's bills? What about all the medicine a sick person has to take? How would your family pay for that?

Many families in the United States do not have to pay all the costs of their health care. Many families have a kind of protection called **insurance** to help them pay their bills. People buy insurance for their cars and for their homes. People also buy **health insurance**, or medical insurance, to help pay for their health care.

The best way to explain insurance is to give an example. Imagine that 20 people get together to form a special group. The purpose of the group is to keep the members from losing money in case of an accident. The group protects, or offers insurance, for their cars the members drive. Each member pays a certain amount of money each month, $20, to save for emergencies.

Imagine that one of the group members, Sally, has a car accident. The damage to her car is $500. The damage to the other car is also $500. Because Sally is a member of the group, she has insurance on her car. The group pays to fix Sally's car and the other car. Sally does not have to pay the entire cost to fix both cars by herself.

This simple example helps explain how insurance works. People pay a certain amount of money each month for protection. Robert's father pays $75 each month for the family's health insurance. Robert's father buys his health insurance through his job as a teacher. The insurance is **affordable** to him because it costs less than if he bought it himself. Because he has health insurance, Robert's father does not have to pay all of the medical bills for his operation. The insurance company helps pay the bills.

There are different kinds of health insurance. Different kinds of insurance have different **coverage**, or services they will pay for. Most types of health insurance help pay for doctors, medicines, hospital stays, tests, and operations. Usually, health insurance will not pay for long-term health care such as a nursing home.

If possible, families should have some kind of health insurance. If a family does not have enough health insurance, they may have financial problems. They may not be able to pay all the doctor's and hospital bills if a family member becomes sick.

Think About It

1. What is health insurance?

   _____

   _____

2. Why is it important for a family to have health insurance?

   _____

   _____

What Does Health Insurance Pay For?

Think about the last time you were sick. Your parent or guardian probably took you to a doctor. The doctor took your temperature and listened to your heart. Your doctor may have taken an X-ray and a sample of blood to test. The doctor probably gave you medicine to take to get well. It takes time and people to help you feel better when you are sick. All these things cost money. Health insurance helps pay for many of these things.

Most kinds of health insurance pay for visits to a doctor when you are sick. Some kinds of insurance also help pay for visits to a doctor when you are well. Many people see their doctors each year to get a physical exam. This exam lets people know if they are healthy. They find out if they have any health problems. They also find out how to stay healthy and avoid becoming sick.

Health insurance will help pay for an **injury** you might get. You might get hurt or injured in an accident at home or in a car. Sometimes you injure yourself playing sports or doing other physical activities.

Sometimes when you are sick or injured, you need to go to the hospital. At the hospital, doctors and nurses do tests to find out what is wrong with you. They also take care of you day and night while you are in the hospital. Health insurance covers the costs of the hospital room, the tests that are done, the medicine you are given, and the care provided by the doctors and nurses.

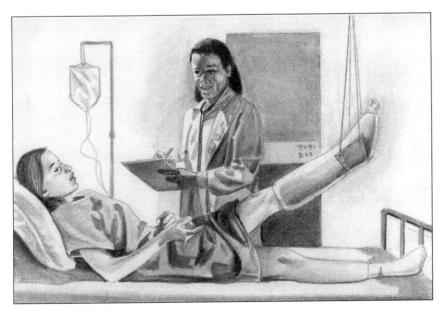

Health insurance will help pay for the costs of caring for an injury.

If you are sick or injured, you might need medicine. Health insurance usually pays for some of the medicine you need to take.

Pregnant women and their unborn babies need special health care. Women should see their doctor often when they are pregnant. The doctor makes sure the unborn child is healthy and strong. The mother also can learn how to take care of herself and her baby. Health insurance will often cover this special care for a woman and her unborn baby.

Some kinds of health insurance also pay for special kinds of health care. For example, people sometimes need to see a doctor for their emotional or mental health. Other kinds of health insurance help pay the costs of seeing a dentist to take care of your teeth. Some kinds of health insurance even pay to see an eye doctor if you need glasses.

Some kinds of health insurance cover unusual or very special needs. These kinds of insurance can be very expensive, but they are available if people need them.

Insurance Basics in Action

3. What are three things that health insurance helps pay for?

_____

_____

_____

4. Why is it important for a pregnant woman to visit her doctor often before her baby is born?

_____

_____

Lesson Review

5. What costs are not usually covered by health insurance?

_____

_____

6. How are people able to get affordable insurance coverage?

_____

_____

7. Imagine a member of your family becomes seriously sick and has to spend 2 weeks in the hospital. What problems might your family have if they do not have health insurance?

_____

_____

_____

Vocabulary Review

On the lines below, write a definition for each vocabulary word.

8. insurance

_____

_____

_____

9. health insurance

_____

_____

_____

10. injury

_____

_____

11. coverage

_____

_____

Portfolio

What Would You Say?

12. Work with a partner. Imagine your partner and his or her family do not have health insurance. Your friend's father thinks health insurance is a waste of money. What would you say to your friend to help him or her understand why health insurance is important? Write a skit explaining to your friend why his or her family should have health insurance.

Health Insurance Options

Some people get health insurance from their workplace. A group insurance plan from work can cover the whole family.

Lesson Objectives

You will be able to

- identify different ways to get health insurance.
- compare the costs of group and individual insurance plans.

Words to Know

employer	person or company for which you work
employee benefit	something an employer provides, such as a paid vacation or health insurance, in addition to your salary
group insurance plan	plan purchased by a group that covers many people and lowers the cost of health insurance
COBRA	plan that allows you to continue your health insurance for a certain time if you lose your job
individual insurance plan	plan purchased by an individual for one person and his or her family
waiting period	time between when you start a job and when your insurance coverage begins
pre-existing condition	health problem a person has before he or she buys health insurance; may delay the start of insurance coverage

Jacob was very excited. He couldn't wait to get home to talk to his wife Olivia and son David.

"Olivia!" Jacob called as he entered the small apartment. "I have some great news for you!"

"Calm down," said Olivia, sitting next to David. "What's gotten into you today?"

"I got the job!" said Jacob with a big smile on his face. "They called me this afternoon."

"That's great news, Jacob," said Olivia. "I know you've wanted this job for a long time. When do you start?"

"I start on Monday," said Jacob. "The job is everything I've wanted. And that's not all. The best part is that we get health insurance. Remember how much it cost last year when David was sick? Now we don't have to worry about doctor bills."

"Jacob, that's great," said Olivia. "It's nice not to have to worry about paying for a doctor when we need to see one. How long do we have to wait to use the health insurance?"

"We only have to wait until the first of the month," said Jacob. "Get your coats, you two. Let's go celebrate."

How You Get Health Insurance

Right now, you are most likely covered by your parents' or guardian's health insurance. You probably will be covered by that insurance until you are 19 or 21 years old. In some cases, you might be covered as long as you are a full-time student at a college or university. But after that time, you will need to get your own health insurance.

You may be wondering why Jacob is so excited about getting health insurance with his new job. In many jobs, health insurance is an **employee benefit**. It is an important benefit to look for when you are searching for a job. An employee benefit is almost like getting extra money for the work you do. Employee benefits include a paid vacation and paid holidays. Another employee benefit is health insurance at a lower cost or no cost to you.

Health insurance is very expensive to buy. You will learn more about these costs in Lessons 5 and 6. One of the best ways to get affordable health insurance is through your **employer**. Your employer is the person or company for which you work.

When you get health insurance from your employer, you are taking part in a group insurance plan. A **group insurance plan** is one that covers health costs for many people. Buying insurance through a group plan lowers the cost to the individuals covered by the plan.

Employers and employees share costs

Most employers help to pay the cost of health insurance for their employees. For example, insurance may cost $200 each month for each employee. The company might pay $150 for each employee. The employee then has to pay only $50 each month. The table on this page shows how much this employee can save on health insurance each year.

Yearly Insurance Costs for One Employee		
Total Cost	Company Pays	Employee Pays
$200 per month	$150 per month	$50 per month
×12 months	×12 months	×12 months
$2,400 per year	$1,800 per year	$600 per year

The table above shows that the employee at this company saves $1,800 per year on health insurance. Now you can see why health insurance is such an important employee benefit.

Some employees pay more for health insurance than others. Marilyn, for example, is not married and she does not have any children. She pays $50 a month for her health insurance. The cost of Jacob's health insurance will be $175 per month. He is paying for himself, his wife Olivia, and his son David.

The amount of money an employee pays for his or her health insurance also depends on the company for which he or she works. The more people that work for a company, the lower the costs of health insurance. Some companies, although not very many, pay the entire cost of an employee's health insurance. The employee pays nothing. That is a great employee benefit!

As long as Jacob has his job, he will have the health insurance provided by his employer. But what happens if Jacob loses his job? What happens to his health insurance?

In 1985, the United States government passed a law to help people who lose their jobs but want to continue their health insurance. This law is called **COBRA**. COBRA works only for a person who has worked for an employer with 20 or more employees. In such a case, the person who loses his or her job can continue his or her health insurance. COBRA allows the person to pay for health insurance under the employer's group plan for up to 18 months. This gives the person time to find other health insurance. Insurance under COBRA costs more than insurance for employees.

Who is covered by a group health insurance plan?

When Jacob started his new job, he was automatically covered by the company's health insurance plan. This is true for most group plans you get through your job. In some unusual cases, a person may not be covered by the group health insurance offered through an employer. These cases are rare. When you start a new job, be sure to find out all you can about your company's health insurance plan.

Like Jacob, you usually have to wait a short time before your health insurance begins. Sometimes, health insurance begins the day you start your job. Most likely, you will have to wait 30 to 60 days from the time you begin your job. Or, you might have to wait until the beginning of the month that follows the date you start your job. This short period of time before your insurance begins is the **waiting period**.

Think About It

1. Why is health insurance an important employee benefit?

   _____

   _____

2. What is a group insurance plan?

   _____

   _____

Buying Your Own Health Insurance

Sometimes, a person cannot buy health insurance through a group insurance plan. Maybe the person works for himself or herself. Maybe the person does not belong to any kind of group that offers a group insurance plan. That person will have to buy his or her own health insurance. This kind of health insurance is called an **individual insurance plan**. An individual insurance plan is sometimes called private health insurance.

A person can buy individual health insurance from more than 2,000 different companies. The prices for the insurance change from company to company. But the prices all have one thing in common. They are expensive. The table on page 12 compares costs of group and individual health insurance. It also includes costs under COBRA.

Cost of Health Insurance Each Month			
Number of People	Group Health	COBRA	Individual Health
single adult	$50	$150	$300
two adults	$75	$175	$400
one adult and one child	$100	$200	$600
two adults and one child	$175	$400	$1,000
two adults and two children	$225	$500	$1,250

Remember Marilyn, the single woman who paid $50 a month for health insurance through her company. As an individual, Marilyn might have to pay as much as $300 a month for health insurance. If Jacob had to buy individual health insurance for himself and his family, he might have to pay $1,000 a month or more for health insurance.

Almost every person can buy individual health insurance if they can afford it. In some unusual cases, however, a person cannot buy health insurance—even if he or she can pay for the insurance. A person might have a serious health problem such as cancer or heart disease. The person may have the health problem before he or she tries to buy insurance. This kind of health problem is called a **pre-existing condition**. An insurance company may choose not to provide health insurance for that person. Or the start of the health insurance may be delayed.

In most cases, you can buy individual health insurance without too much trouble. You first need to apply for the health insurance. You may have to take a physical examination from a doctor. The insurance company wants to know how healthy you are before they let you buy health insurance. You may also have to fill out a form that tells your medical, or health, history. You will learn more about applying for health insurance in Lesson 3.

Insurance Basics in Action

3. What is an individual insurance plan?

_____

_____

4. Compare the costs of a group insurance plan to an individual insurance plan.

_____

_____

Lesson Review

Answer the following questions on the lines provided.

5. What is COBRA? How does COBRA help a person keep his or her health insurance?

_____

_____

_____

6. Who can be covered by a group health insurance plan provided by an employer?

_____

_____

Vocabulary Review

Write the letter of the definition from Column 2 on the line in front of the correct term in Column 1.

Column 1	Column 2
_____ **7.** employer	**a.** health problem a person has before he or she buys health insurance; may delay start of insurance
_____ **8.** employee benefits	**b.** health insurance purchased by an individual for one person and his or her family
_____ **9.** group insurance plan	**c.** time before your insurance coverage begins
_____ **10.** COBRA	**d.** person or company you work for
_____ **11.** individual insurance plan	**e.** things an employer provides, such as paid vacation and health insurance, in addition to your salary
_____ **12.** waiting period	**f.** plan that allows you to continue your health insurance if you lose your job
_____ **13.** pre-existing condition	**g.** plan that covers many people and lowers the cost of health insurance

Portfolio

What Would You Do?

14. Imagine you have been offered two jobs. The first job pays more money a year but has no employee benefits. You must buy your own health insurance. The second job pays less, but it offers group health insurance. Which job would you take? Write the reasons for your decision in your journal.

Applying for Health Insurance

Your medical history is a record of your health care. It is important to know your medical history if you are getting health insurance.

Lesson Objectives

You will be able to
- describe your medical history.
- gather the information needed to apply for health insurance.

Words To Know

medical history   record of your health from the time you were born to the present

social security number   identification number given to a person by the United States government

vaccination   shot to protect you from getting a certain disease

allergic, allergy   having a bad reaction such as a rash, upset stomach, itchy watery eyes and nose, or trouble breathing; usually caused by something you eat, touch, or breathe

Farah was leaving home for the summer. She had a job as a camp counselor in a different state.

"Mom," asked Farah, "the camp wants to know my medical history. What is that?"

"What do you think it is?" asked Farah's mother. "Just stop and think about it for a minute."

"Well," thought Farah, "it kind of sounds like the history of my health. You know, if and when I was sick, if I had any shots, that kind of thing. Am I right?"

"You're right as far as you went," answered Farah's mom. "What other kinds of things do you think the camp might want to know about your health? Let's look at the form they sent you."

Farah and her mother studied the form the camp sent. With her mother's help, Farah began to write her medical history.

Your Medical History

Farah was doing an important thing. She was learning all about her **medical history**. Your medical history is a record of your health—both good and bad—from the time you were born to the present. Farah needs her medical history for her summer job. You will need to know your medical history if you are buying health insurance. Most insurance companies ask you to fill out a form that tells your medical history. The form also has some other information about you.

The first thing on the form is a place for your name, address, and telephone number. If you are under 18 years old, the form will also ask for the names of your parents or guardian.

The form also asks for your **social security number**. Almost every person in the United States has a social security number. This number is an identification number given to a person by the United States government. Some parents fill out the forms for a social security number when their children are born. You can also apply for a number yourself at the local Social Security office. You'll need a copy of your birth certificate to get a social security number.

A person has the same social security number for his or her entire life. You need this number to get a job, to get a driver's license, and to open a bank account. You need a social security number to pay taxes. You also need a social security number to buy health insurance.

You have the same social security number for your entire life.

The rest of the insurance application form asks about your medical history. You will probably need to answer questions such as the following:

- What **vaccinations** have you had? A vaccination is a shot to protect you from getting a certain disease. When you were a baby, you probably had vaccinations for diseases such as whooping cough and tetanus.

- What childhood diseases have you had? Many children have diseases such as measles, chicken pox, and mumps when they are young.

- Have you ever been in the hospital? If so, what for? You may have been in the hospital if you were sick or injured. You may have had an operation to remove your tonsils or appendix. If you injured yourself playing, you might have been to the hospital to set a broken bone.

- Are you **allergic** to any medicines? Sometimes people have a bad reaction when they take certain kinds of medicine. They are allergic to the medicine. It is important to know if you have an **allergy**, especially to any kinds of medicines.

The form might ask questions about other members of your family. Some diseases, such as cancer and heart disease, seem to be common in some families. The form also will ask if you smoke cigarettes, if you have taken any kinds of drugs, and if you drink alcohol.

Your parents or guardian will probably know most of the information you need to complete your medical history. Sometimes, however, you will need to get the information from your doctor. Most teenagers under 18 years old will need to get a signature from their parent or guardian to get their medical records. Sometimes, you can get the information you need by calling your doctor. You may need to write your doctor a letter asking questions about the information you need.

Think About It

1. Why is it important to know your medical history?

_____

_____

2. How do you find the information you need to write your medical history?

_____

_____

Lesson Review

Answer the following questions on the lines provided.

3. What is a social security number?

_____

_____

4. Why do you need a social security number?

_____

_____

5. What kinds of information do you need to apply for health insurance?

_____

_____

_____

Vocabulary Review

On the lines below, write a sentence using each vocabulary word correctly.

6. medical history

_____

_____

7. social security number

_____

_____

8. vaccination

_____

_____

Portfolio

What Would You Do?

9. How might you go about finding out your social security number? What could you do to get one if you didn't have one?

UNIT REVIEW

Take Another Look

Answer the following questions on the lines provided.

1. Why is it important for the girl shown above to have health insurance?

   _____

   _____

2. What kinds of costs might this girl have that health insurance would cover?

   _____

   _____

Cost of Health Insurance Each Month			
Number of People	Group Health	COBRA	Individual Health
single adult	$50	$150	$300
family	$225	$500	$1,250

3. Look at the chart above. Compare the plans for a single adult. How much more does individual health insurance cost than group health insurance?

   _____

   _____

4. Why do you think family insurance costs so much more than individual insurance?

   _____

   _____

Reviewing What You Know

5. Name three important things about health insurance.

_____

_____

6. Why is it important for a family to have health insurance?

_____

_____

7. What are two ways in which a person can buy health insurance?

_____

_____

_____

8. Why is it important to know your medical history?

_____

_____

Complete the following sentences.

9. Your _____ is an identification number given to you by the United States government.

10. If you have a(n) _____ before you try to buy health insurance, you may not be able to get insurance or the start of your coverage may be delayed.

11. The name of the plan that lets you continue your health insurance if you lose your job is _____.

Cooperative Learning

12. Work with three of your classmates. In the yellow pages of the telephone book, look up the names and addresses of four companies that sell health insurance. Write a letter to each company and ask them for basic information about the health insurance they offer. Ask if they sell individual health insurance. Ask for the cost of the insurance. How much does it cost for one adult, two adults, and a family? Find out if there are any pre-existing conditions that would keep a person from buying the health insurance. Summarize the information you get on a poster to share with the rest of the class.

13. Work with a partner. Imagine that one of you is an insurance agent and the other is a customer who wants to buy health insurance. Role-play a telephone conversation where the customer asks questions about health insurance and the agent answers the customer's questions.

Lesson 4

How Do Payments Work?

The cost of health insurance depends on the number of family members who are being insured.

Lesson Objectives

You will be able to

- explain how people pay for monthly and yearly costs of health insurance.
- describe how copayments and coinsurance are calculated and paid.

Words to Know

coinsurance	amount of your health care costs you pay after the insurance company pays, not including the deductible
copayment	fixed dollar amount you pay for a specific health care service, such as a visit to a doctor's office
out-of-pocket limit	greatest amount of money you pay for health care in one year; point at which insurance pays 100 percent
premium	the amount of money you pay each month to have health insurance
reasonable and customary costs	standard charges for health care; costs above this are not covered by insurance
yearly deductible	the amount you must spend each year before the insurance company pays anything

Marcella had been home from the hospital for two weeks. Her and Michael's new baby was only sixteen days old.

"What are you doing, Michael?" asked Marcella. "Come see our beautiful new son. I think he's smiling."

"I'll be right there," said Michael. "I just have to pay one more hospital bill."

"I can hardly believe how much it costs to have a baby," said Marcella. "It sure is a good thing we have health insurance to help pay those bills."

"We're really lucky," answered Michael. "And now that we have the baby, our health insurance will also cover him. And if any of us get sick, we'll only have to pay a small part of the total costs—not the whole thing."

Paying for Health Insurance

As you learned in earlier lessons, paying for health insurance can be very expensive. The most affordable way to buy health insurance is through a group insurance plan. Even if you belong to a group insurance plan, you still have to pay something for your health insurance.

Remember the company in Lesson 2 that gives health insurance as an employee benefit? The company pays $150 each month and the employee pays $50. The amount of money a person or a company pays each month for health insurance is the **premium**.

The amount of the premium is different from plan to plan. It depends on the kind of insurance you have. It also depends on the number of people who belong to the same insurance plan. The more people who belong to a group insurance plan, the lower the monthly premiums.

The premium also depends on the number of family members who are insured. A single person pays a smaller premium each month than two adults, or a married man or woman with children. Look at the chart in the margin. Notice how the premium changes for the number of family members being insured.

Monthly Premiums	
single adult	$50
two adults	$75
one adult, one child	$100
two adults, two children	$225

Insurance Basics in Action

1. A person or a company pays a _____ each month for health insurance.

2. The more people that belong to a group insurance plan, the _____ the monthly premiums.

What are yearly deductibles?

Paying a monthly premium is not the end of your health care costs. Almost all kinds of health insurance ask you to spend some money up front before they start paying part of your bills.

Most health insurance plans make you pay a yearly deductible. A **yearly deductible** is the amount you must spend on health care each year before the insurance company begins to pay part of your bills.

Health insurance deductibles are different for different people. Look at the chart in the margin. A single person, for example, has only one deductible. Let's say that amount is $100 a year. A married couple has an additional deductible. Their deductible is $100 for each person each year, or a total deductible of $200. What about a married couple with three children? The deductible for each person is $100 each year or a total of $500 for the whole family.

How does a deductible work? Imagine that your deductible is $100 per year. You are sick and have to go to the doctor. The cost of your visit to the doctor's office is $50. You also have blood tests that cost $50. The doctor also gives you medicine that costs $20. The total cost of the doctor visit, the blood tests, and medicine is $120. Your deductible is $100. You have paid $20 more than the amount of your deductible. Your health insurance will now begin paying for your health care.

Yearly Deductibles	
single adult	$100
married couple	$200
family (three children)	$500

Think About It

3. What is a yearly deductible?

_____

_____

Paying Health Care Costs

Even after you've paid your deductible, your health insurance still does not pay all the costs of your health care. Most insurance companies still ask you to pay part of your health care costs. Let's go back to our example.

You have paid $120 this year for your visit to the doctor, blood tests, and some medicine. Your deductible is $100 each year. You have paid $20 more than the amount of your deductible ($120 − $100 = $20). What happens to the money you paid over your deductible? You get part of that money back from the insurance company.

What are coinsurance and copayments?

Your health insurance also includes coinsurance. **Coinsurance** is the amount of your health care costs that are shared with the insurance company after the deductible is paid. Once you have paid your deductible for the year, you and the insurance company share your remaining health care costs for the year. For any amount over the deductible, most insurance companies pay 80 percent. You have to pay the remaining 20 percent. Let's go back to our example.

You have paid $20 more than the amount of your deductible. So the insurance company owes you money. The insurance company will pay 80 percent of $20 back to you. Look at the example on this page.

Example	
Doctor's visit	$50
Blood tests	$50
Medicine	+$20
Total cost for health care	$120
Amount of deductible	–$100
Amount you paid over deductible	$20
80% paid by insurance	$20 × 80% = $16
20% paid by you as coinsurance	$20 × 20% = $4

You have spent a total of $104. This is the sum of the $100 deductible plus $4 coinsurance.

Some health insurance plans also have a **copayment**. A copayment is the amount of money you pay for a certain health care service. For example, with some health insurance you only have to pay $10 each time you visit the doctor. This amount is the copayment. Another example of a copayment is paying only $15 each time you get medicine, no matter what the cost. Health insurance that has copayments, still has a yearly deductible.

Insurance Basics in Action

4. What is coinsurance? What percent of the costs will insurance companies usually pay?

_____

5. How do copayments help you save money on medicines?

_____

_____

How much will your health insurance pay?

Imagine that you still did not feel well. You went back to see your doctor, and he decided you had to go to the hospital for an operation.

Remember you have already paid your $100 yearly deductible. Any costs over the $100 will be shared by you and the insurance company. The insurance company will pay 80 percent. You will pay 20 percent. Do you have to continue to pay 20 percent of all the costs?

Most health insurance has an **out-of-pocket limit**. After you have paid a certain amount in one year, the insurance company begins to pay 100 percent of your health care costs. The out-of-pocket limit includes the deductible and coinsurance added together.

Imagine that all your doctor's visits and your operation cost $10,000. The out-of-pocket limit for your health insurance is $1,000. Remember you've already paid the $100 deductible. You will have to pay your 20 percent until you have paid a total of $1,000. After you have paid a total of $1,000 ($100 deductible + $900 of coinsurance), the insurance company will pay 100 percent of the remaining costs for that year. In this case, the insurance company pays $9,000 for your health care. Look at the example in the margin.

Many insurance companies also have a maximum charge that they will pay for a particular service. These amounts are called **reasonable and customary costs**. The reasonable and customary costs are different for different areas of the country.

Assume you live in an area where the reasonable and customary cost is $800 for your operation. If your surgeon charges $700, and the insurance company pays 80 percent, or $560, and you pay the rest, $140. If the surgeon charges $800, the insurance company pays 80 percent, or $640 and you pay $160.

However, if the surgeon charges more than $800, you have to pay the difference. The insurance company will pay no more than $640. If the surgeon charges $1,000, you will have to pay $160 plus $200, for a total of $360. Look at the chart below.

Example	
Cost of operation	$10,000
Deductible and coinsurance	−$1,000
Insurance pays	$9,000

$800 Reasonable and Customary Cost		
Doctor's fee	Insurance pays (80%)	You pay (20% +)
$700	$560	$140
$800	$640	$160
$1,000	$640	$360

Lesson Review

6. What does it mean when you reach the out-of-pocket limit on your health insurance policy?

_____

_____

7. Your health insurance has a $250 yearly deductible. Your coinsurance is then 20 percent of your health care costs. If your health care costs were $500 last year, how much did you spend?

_____

8. How are coinsurance and copayments different?

_____

_____

Vocabulary Review

Write the letter of the definition from Column 2 on the line in front of the correct term in Column 1.

Column 1	Column 2
_____ **9.** reasonable and customary costs	**a.** fixed dollar amount you pay for a certain health care service, such as a visit to a doctor's office
_____ **10.** coinsurance	**b.** the amount of money you pay each month to have health insurance
_____ **11.** copayment	**c.** the amount you must spend each year before the insurance company pays anything
_____ **12.** out-of-pocket limit	**d.** the amount of money you must spend before the insurance company pays 100 percent of your health care costs
_____ **13.** premium	**e.** part of health care costs you pay after the deductible is paid
_____ **14.** yearly deductible	**f.** standard charges for health care; costs above are not covered by insurance

Portfolio

What Would You Say?

15. Work with a friend. Imagine that your friend just got a new job. One benefit of the job is health insurance. Your friend thinks the health insurance is free. Write a skit that explains to your friend that he or she has to pay a premium each month for the insurance.

Lesson 5

The Different Types of Plans

It is important to compare different plans before you choose health insurance.

Lesson Objectives

You will be able to

- compare Traditional Care Plans, Managed Care Plans, and HMOs.
- explain networks.

Words to Know

HMO (Health Maintenance Organization)	health insurance plan in which your health care needs are covered through a network only
in-network	going to doctors, nurses, or hospitals that are part of a network
Managed Care Plan	kind of health insurance in which you may choose the doctor or you may use a network; helps control the cost of health care
network	group of doctors and hospitals that provide health care at a lower cost to its members
out-of-network	going to doctors, nurses, or hospitals that are not part of a network
preventive care	seeing a doctor while you are healthy to prevent becoming sick
Traditional Care Plan	kind of health insurance in which you choose the doctors you see

Roberta has a new job. She is the assistant to the manager of the new department store. Today is her first day at work. The first thing she has to do is talk to someone about health insurance. Health insurance is one of the benefits of Roberta's new job.

"Welcome to the company," said Mr. Miller. "I'm sure you'll like it here."

"Thank you, Mr. Miller," said Roberta. "I'm excited about starting my first real job."

"Good, let's get started," said Mr. Miller. "Health insurance is one of your benefits."

"I know," said Roberta. "I'm happy about that. I know a little bit about how much health insurance costs."

"That's good information to have," said Mr. Miller. "Did you know that the company offers three different kinds of health insurance? You can choose the one that fits your needs the best."

"I didn't know there were different kinds of health insurance," said Roberta. "How will I ever know which one is right for me?"

"That's why I'm here," answered Mr. Miller. "I'll explain the different plans to you. Then you can make your choice."

What Are the Different Kinds of Health Insurance?

Like Roberta, you may think that all kinds of health insurance are the same. And like Roberta, you are probably surprised to find out there are different kinds of health insurance. Let's look at the differences in kinds of health insurance.

The first kind of health insurance available is called a **Traditional Care Plan**. In this kind of health insurance, you make most of your own choices about your health care. A good thing, or an advantage, of this plan is that you can see any doctor whenever you want.

Another advantage of a Traditional Care Plan is that you and your doctor decide if you need to go to a hospital. You also decide which hospital to go to.

With this kind of insurance, you usually pay your doctor yourself. You then have to fill out paperwork to send to your insurance company. Your insurance company then pays you back for the costs of your health care. Sometimes a doctor will send his or her bill directly to the insurance company.

To cover the costs of a Traditional Care Plan, you pay a monthly premium and a yearly deductible. The insurance company pays for a large percent of the rest of your health care.

A bad thing, or disadvantage, is that this kind of health insurance is quite expensive. Employers want to provide the best health insurance possible for their employees. This means keeping the costs down. Employers now have other kinds of health insurance they can provide their employees. These kinds of insurance help keep the costs down—both for the employer and the employee.

Think About It

1. What is a Traditional Care Plan?

   _____

   _____

   _____

2. How do you pay for health care costs when you have a Traditional Care Plan?

   _____

   _____

Lowering the costs of health care

One way employers lower the cost of health insurance is to provide insurance that controls the cost of health care. Most of these lower costing plans use a **network**. You probably know that a television network is a group of TV stations that work together to broadcast programs. In health care, a network is a group of doctors and hospitals that provide health care at a lower cost to its members. The doctors and hospitals in the network often agree on the costs of certain kinds of health care. The insurance company then agrees to pay the doctors and hospitals a certain amount of money.

There are two kinds of health insurance that use a network. The first kind is called a **Health Maintenance Organization**, or **HMO** for short. An HMO is a kind of plan in which members are covered for most health care needs. HMOs work with a network of doctors and hospitals. In an HMO only costs that are **in-network** are covered. That means you must see doctors and go to hospitals that are part of the network or your insurance company will not pay.

If you belong to an HMO, you must choose one doctor from the network. You see that doctor for most of your health care needs. If you are sick or injured, you see the doctor you chose from the network. If you need to see another doctor for special treatment, your doctor will make the arrangements for you. You cannot see another doctor any time you want. If you need to go to a hospital, you can only go to the hospitals that are part of the HMO's network.

One reason for choosing an HMO is that they are very affordable. They have low premiums and they usually have low copayments. Another reason for choosing an HMO is preventive care. **Preventive care** is just what it sounds like. It is seeing a doctor and taking care of yourself while you are healthy to prevent becoming sick.

Another kind of health insurance is called a **Managed Care Plan**. A Managed Care Plan is similar to an HMO. It has a network of doctors and hospitals. If you belong to a Managed Care Plan instead of an HMO, however, you can go **out-of-network**. This means you can choose to see any doctor you want and part of the cost will be paid by insurance. But, it will cost you less if you choose a doctor from the network. The same is true about hospitals. You can go to any hospital when you need to, but the cost is less if you go to a hospital in the network.

Comparing the three types of plans

One of the biggest differences between the plans involves preventive care. With an HMO, preventive care is usually covered. With a Managed Care Plan, only some preventive care is covered. With a Traditional Care Plan, most preventive care is not covered.

People like to choose HMOs or Managed Care Plans, because health insurance costs are usually much less than with a Traditional Care Plan. With an HMO, your only costs are the low copayments you make when you see a doctor. With a Managed Care Plan, your costs are lower if you choose a doctor or hospital from within the network. If you choose a doctor or hospital that is not part of the network, your costs will be higher.

Many people do not like HMOs for one simple reason. They must use a doctor that is part of the HMO's network. For some people, being able to choose their own doctor is worth the extra cost of a Traditional Care Plan.

The chart on page 30 compares the advantages and disadvantages of Traditional Care Plans, HMOs, and Managed Care Plans.

Compare Health Insurance Plans			
Kind of Plan	Advantages	Disadvantages	Cost to Individual
Traditional Care	• choose any doctor at any time • can go to any hospital	• often lots of paperwork • little or no preventive care	• high premiums • pays 80%–90% of costs
Managed Care	• may choose any doctor or hospital • some preventive care • can be in-network or out-of-network	• preventive care not always covered	• medium premiums • pays 60%–70% out-of-network • low copayment in-network
HMO	• most preventive care covered • very little paperwork	• cannot use doctor or hospital outside HMO network	• low premiums • low copayments

Insurance Basics in Action

3. If you see a doctor to get _____ , you are trying to stay healthy and keep from becoming sick.

4. In a Managed Care Plan, seeing a doctor from a _____ can help save you money on health care.

5. In a(n) _____ your health care costs are not covered if you go out-of-network.

Lesson Review

6. What is one advantage of belonging to an HMO? What is one disadvantage?

   _____

   _____

7. What are the advantages of using doctors and hospitals from a network when you belong to a Managed Care Plan?

   _____

   _____

   _____

8. Why do some people choose to pay the higher costs of a Traditional Care Plan?

_____

_____

Vocabulary Review

Write the letter of the definition from Column 2 on the line in front of the correct term in Column 1.

Column 1	Column 2
____ **9.** Traditional Care Plan	**a.** going to doctors, nurses or hospitals from a network
____ **10.** in-network	**b.** kind of health insurance plan where you can choose doctors and hospitals from a network or not
____ **11.** Managed Care Plan	**c.** seeing a doctor while you are healthy to prevent becoming sick
____ **12.** network	**d.** going to doctors, nurses, or hospitals that are not part of a network
____ **13.** HMO	**e.** kind of health insurance plan in which you choose the doctors you see
____ **14.** preventive care	**f.** kind of health insurance plan in which your health care costs are covered by a network only
____ **15.** out-of-network	**g.** group of doctors and hospitals that provide health care at a lower cost to its members

Portfolio

What Would You Say?

16. Imagine that you have a friend. Your friend has a good job and can afford to buy a Traditional Care Plan. Your friend has been going to the same doctor for 25 years. Your friend trusts and likes her doctor very much. What would you tell your friend about HMOs if she wanted to buy a different kind of health insurance? What would you tell her about Managed Care Plans?

Comparing Plans

People should compare the costs of different insurance plans. This helps people decide what kind of health insurance is best for them.

Lesson Objectives

You will be able to

- compare the costs of different insurance plans.
- decide which kind of health insurance is best for you.

Word to Know

options things that can be chosen

Roberta finished her first day at her new job. She was tired and excited. She needed to make a decision about her health insurance by the end of the week.

"What are you doing?" asked Roberta's father. "I'd thought you would be tired after your first day of work."

"I am, Dad," answered Roberta. "But I have a decision to make."

"Can I help in some way?" asked Roberta's dad.

"Maybe you can," said Roberta. "I need to decide which kind of health insurance I want. I need to make up my mind by the end of the week."

"Let's look at what you have here," said Roberta's father. "We'll compare the plans and then find out how much they cost."

"That sounds like a plan to me," said Roberta. "Let's get started. I have a feeling this will take a long time."

Choosing the Right Health Insurance

Roberta really took some time to review her **options**, the plans from which she could choose. Choosing a health insurance plan can be difficult and confusing.

Roberta had three choices of health insurance from her employer. One choice was a Traditional Care Plan. The second choice was an HMO. The third choice was a Managed Care Plan. Roberta studied all of her options.

She and her family were new in town. They had not even seen a doctor since they moved. They lived close to the center of town. They were not too far away from the city's hospitals. Roberta noticed many doctor's offices on the bus route to her new job. Choosing a specific doctor or hospital was not too important to Roberta.

She had always been healthy and active. She liked the idea of having preventive care to keep her healthy.

Roberta and her father looked through all the health plans. Roberta decided that an HMO might be the best kind of health insurance for her.

But then her father asked the big question. How much will it cost? The three kinds of health insurance—Traditional Care Plan, HMO, and Managed Care Plan—cost different amounts. How do they compare?

Roberta really took some time to review her **options**, the plans from which she could choose. Choosing a health insurance plan can be difficult and confusing.

Roberta had three choices of health insurance from her employer. One choice was a Traditional Care Plan. The second choice was an HMO. The third choice was a Managed Care Plan. Roberta studied all of her options.

Roberta's Chart: Compare Costs of Three Plans			
Costs	Traditional Care Plan	HMO	Managed Care Plan

Monthly premium
  one person
  two people
  family
	$60
	$100
	$175
		$30
		$75
		$225
			$50
			$100
			$175

Yearly deductible	$100 per person	$100 per person	$100 per person
Doctor's visits	80% paid	$10 copayment	$10 copayment if in-network; 70% paid if out-of-network
Hospital stay	80% paid	$100 copayment	$150 copayment if in-network; 70% paid if out-of-network
Preventive care	none	100% paid	$15 copayment if in-network; none if out-of-network
Out-of-pocket limit	$2,000 per year	none	$1,000 per year

Insurance Basics in Action

Use the chart above to complete the following sentences.

1. The insurance with the best preventive care is _____ .

2. The insurance with the highest yearly out-of-pocket limit is _____
_____ .

3. The insurance with the lowest monthly premium for one person is _____
_____ .

Lesson Review

Use Roberta's chart on page 34 to answer the following questions.

4. Which kind of insurance in Roberta's chart costs the most for one person for one year?

_____

5. Which kind of insurance in Roberta's chart do you think would be the best for a married couple to buy? Why?

_____

_____

_____

6. Which kind of insurance in Roberta's chart do you think would be the best for a family to buy? Why?

_____

_____

_____

7. What things should you look at when you decide on the right health insurance for you?

_____

_____

_____

Portfolio

What Would You Say?

8. Pretend your guardian knows you have been learning the basics of health insurance in school. Your guardian has just started a new job. She asks you to help her select her new health insurance. Write a list of questions your guardian should ask her employer about her health insurance.

UNIT REVIEW

Take Another Look

The following table shows the advantages and disadvantages of different kinds of health insurance. Fill in the blanks in the table.

Kinds of Health Insurance	
Kind of plan	(1) _____
Advantages	• choose any doctor at any time • can go to any hospital
Disadvantages	• often lots of paperwork • little or no **(2)** _____
Costs to Individual	• high **(3)** _____ • pays 80-90% of costs
Kind of plan	Managed Care
Advantages	• may choose **(4)** _____ • some preventive care • can be in-network or out-of-network
Disadvantages	• preventive care **(5)** _____
Costs to Individual	• medium premiums • pays 60%–70% out-of-network • low copayment in-network
Kind of plan	(6) _____
Advantages	• most preventive care covered • very little paperwork
Disadvantages	• cannot use doctor or hospital **(7)** _____
Costs to Individual	• **(8)** _____ premiums • low copayments

Reviewing What You Know

9. What are the differences between a Managed Care Plan and an HMO?

_____

_____

_____

10. How much of your health care costs does health insurance pay once you reach the out-of-pocket limit?

_____

_____

11. How does a network try to lower the costs of health care?

_____

_____

Complete the following sentences.

12. The choices you have among health insurance plans are called your _____ .

13. The _____ is the amount of money you must spend each year before the insurance company begins paying anything toward your health care.

14. A(n) _____ is a group of doctors and hospitals that provide health care at a lower cost to its members.

15. The kind of health insurance in which a person can choose to see any doctor at any time is called _____ .

Cooperative Learning

16. Work with a partner. Look at the information in Roberta's chart on page 34. Get a copy of a health insurance policy from your teacher. Find out the costs for the same information in Roberta's chart. Compare what the costs would be for your family and your partner's family for this health insurance. For which family would health insurance cost less?

17. Work with a partner. Write a list of questions you would like to know about HMOs. Then get a copy of an HMO plan or policy from your teacher. Use the information in the policy to find the answers to your questions.

Lesson 7

Doctors, Hospitals, & Emergencies

How do people go about picking a doctor? One thing that people can do is ask doctors questions about how they care for people.

Lesson Objectives

You will be able to

- explain how to choose a primary care physician.

- describe what you must do for hospital and emergency room visits.

Words to Know

emergency	accident or health problem for which you need help right away
emergency room	part of a hospital that provides 24-hour emergency care
precertification	approval from a person's health insurance for a hospital visit; must be approved before the person goes to the hospital
primary care physician	doctor you select from a network; doctor you see for most of your health care needs

Shawna loved her new job. She even had health insurance as an employee benefit. Yesterday, her boss reminded her that she needed to choose a doctor.

"I know I need to choose a doctor," said Shawna. "But how do I do that?"

"Choosing a doctor is an important and difficult decision," said Shawna's boss. "You need to remember that our health insurance plan has a network. Have you looked at that list of doctors yet?"

"No I haven't," answered Shawna. "Do you know any of the doctors on that list?"

"I know several of the doctors on the list," answered Shawna's boss. "Come to think of it, you might like the doctor I go to. Here, let me give you her name."

"Thank you," said Shawna. "Maybe I'll give her a call and talk to her."

Choosing Your Primary Care Physician

How do you go about picking a doctor? Your health insurance may have some say in your decision. If you have a Traditional Care Plan, you can go to any doctor you choose.

If your health plan says you have to pick a doctor, choosing your **primary care physician** can be difficult and confusing. But, it is one of the most important decisions you will make about your health care. Your primary care physician will help make most of your health care decisions. You may have the same doctor for many years. You need to trust and like your doctor.

If you belong to an HMO, you need to choose a doctor from the HMO's network. If you belong to a Managed Care Plan, you can go to any doctor you want. However, if you choose a doctor from the Managed Care Plan's network, your health care costs will be much lower.

Shawna's health insurance is provided by a Managed Care Plan. She took her boss's advice. The first thing she did to choose a primary care physician was look at the list of doctors in the Managed Care Plan's network. Shawna was surprised to find out how many doctors were included.

Shawna has two small children. A friend of Shawna's suggested that Shawna choose a doctor who can take care of both Shawna and her children. Shawna thought that was a good idea.

Shawna knows that she wants her doctor to be a woman. She is more comfortable with a woman doctor than with a man. Shawna also wants a doctor who is easy to talk to. Some doctors are too difficult to understand when they explain things.

Shawna lives in a big city. She wants a doctor whose office is close to her home. The last thing she wants to do is take the bus across town when she or her children are sick.

With these things in mind, Shawna looked at the list again. She found three female family doctors close to her home.

The next thing Shawna did was ask her friends and the people she worked with about the doctors. One of the men Shawna worked with knows one of the doctors. He and his family have been going to the doctor for 10 years. Everyone in the family likes her.

The next thing Shawna did was very important. She called the doctor. She asked if she could make an appointment to meet with the doctor and speak with her. Shawna wanted to find out if she liked the doctor and if she was easy to talk to. Most doctors will make an appointment for you to meet them.

Shawna did all the right things to choose her doctor. She chose a doctor from her Managed Care Plan's network. She decided if she wanted a male or a female doctor. She knew she wanted a doctor to take care of her and her children. She also knew she wanted a doctor close to home. Shawna then asked people she knew about their doctors. Finally, Shawna made an appointment to meet the doctor and ask her questions.

Think About It

1. Why is choosing a primary care physician such an important and difficult decision?

_____

_____

2. Name two things you should do when choosing your primary care physician.

_____

_____

Going to the Hospital

At some time in your life, you may be very sick or have a serious injury. You may need to go to the hospital for treatment. You may need special medicines. Or, you may need an operation to make you well. Your health insurance will pay for the costs of the doctors and nurses, medicines, and the hospital.

If you need to go to the hospital, the health insurance company may be involved in the decision. In most cases, you or your doctor must let the health insurance company know that you are going to the hospital. The doctor must explain why the hospital visit is necessary. This is called **precertification**. A Managed Care Plan or an HMO insurance company will need to approve the hospital visit before you go. This is how they avoid unnecessary stays in the hospital. They are trying to keep down the high costs of health care. Some companies will not pay the hospital costs if they have not approved the visit before you go to the hospital.

For many people, a hospital stay is not necessary. Many kinds of health care can be given in a doctor's office or in a special clinic. The person can go home soon after the treatment is finished.

Insurance Basics in Action

3. Give two health reasons why you may need to go to the hospital.

_____

4. Who might make the decision for a person to go to the hospital?

_____

_____

What to do in an emergency

Sometimes you are faced with a medical **emergency**. An emergency is an accident or health problem for which you need help right away. Emergencies include bleeding that will not stop, an injury to the head, choking, poisoning, and severe burns. Other kinds of health problems are also emergencies. A heart attack is an emergency. If a person is unconscious, or unable to think or feel, it is an emergency.

When you have a medical emergency, you need to get to the nearest **emergency room** as soon as possible. An emergency room is a part of a hospital that gives 24-hour emergency care.

No hospital emergency room can turn away a person who needs medical care. This is true even if the person does not have health insurance. Many emergencies are life or death situations. A person needs care immediately.

If you have a health emergency, go to an emergency room as soon as possible. Then call your insurance company. If you cannot make the call, ask a family member to call for you.

If you have an emergency, go to the nearest emergency room—even if the hospital is not part of the network for your health insurance. If you can get to an emergency room that is part of your health insurance, however, it is easier for both you and your insurance company.

When you get to the emergency room, get the care you need. Then call your insurance company as soon as possible, within 24 to 48 hours is best. If you cannot call yourself, have someone else call for you. You need to let your insurance company know that you are in the hospital and for what reason. Be sure you know the time limit for calling. Some insurance companies will not cover an emergency room visit if you don't call within the time limit.

Your health insurance will usually pay for a visit to an emergency room. You may need to make a copayment or pay your normal coinsurance.

What do you do if you have an emergency when you are away from home? What happens if you are traveling in a foreign country? The first thing to do is get the emergency care you need. Call your insurance company as soon as possible. They will tell you what you need to do. Like you, the health insurance company wants you to get the care you need as soon as possible.

Lesson Review

5. Why does your health insurance company want to know if you are going to the hospital?

_____

_____

6. What should you do if you have a medical emergency?

_____

_____

7. If you have an emergency, when should you call your health insurance company?

_____

_____

Vocabulary Review

Write a definition for each vocabulary word on the lines provided.

8. emergency

_____

_____

9. emergency room

_____

_____

10. precertification

_____

_____

Portfolio

What Would You Say?

11. Work with a partner. Imagine your friend was making lunch. He burned his finger on the stove. The burn was not serious. Your friend wanted to go to the emergency room to have his finger taken care of. You tell your friend to go to the doctor instead. Write a skit that explains why your friend should not go to the emergency room.

Filing a Claim

You must file a claim form in order to use your health insurance.

Lesson Objectives

You will be able to

- complete a claim form for health care costs.

- read an Explanation of Benefits Statement.

Words to Know

claim	form for the insurance company that must be completed by you and the doctor; it describes the kind of health care you received
dependent	someone, usually a child, that an adult is responsible for
explanation of benefits statement	a form that the insurance company sends to you to show how your health care costs are being paid
file a claim	to fill out a claim form completely and correctly, then send the form and the doctor's bills to your insurance company
doctor's bill	a list from the doctor showing what was wrong with you, what was done, and how much it cost
identification card	card you get from your employer that identifies you as a member of the group health insurance plan
marital status	tells whether you are single or married

Edward had not been feeling well. He missed two days of work. He called his boss and said he was going to the doctor.

"Good, but before you go to the doctor, see Carol in the office," said Edward's boss. "She will give you a form to fill out. You should take the form with you to the doctor when you go."

"What kind of form should I get from Carol?" asked Edward.

"It's called a claim form," said Edward's boss. "Just tell Carol you need it to see the doctor. She'll know what to give you."

"Thanks," said Edward. "I'll do that."

How to File a Claim

Edward had never used his health insurance before. He asked Carol for a **claim** form. A claim is a form that must be completed by you and sometimes your doctor that describes the kind of health care you received. The claim must be completed before the health insurance pays money to you or your doctor.

Carol gave Edward the claim form. She told him to fill out the first half. She also told him to take the form to his doctor's office. The doctor may fill out more information on the claim form. Or the doctor may give you a **doctor's bill**. This tells each thing the doctor did, the cost, and what the doctor thinks is wrong with you. The doctor may mail the completed form to the health insurance company for you.

But just what is a claim form? The figure on page 46 shows an example of a claim form. All claim forms are a little different, but most of them ask for the same basic information. Look at the form as you read how to **file a claim**. When you "file a claim" you fill out the claim form completely and correctly. Send the form and doctor's bills to your insurance company. Remember, keep copies of anything you send to the insurance company.

If your claim is not filed correctly, the insurance company may not pay the doctor or hospital for your health care. An incorrectly filed claim will always slow down the payment to the doctor or hospital. It will also slow down a payment back to you.

Think About It

1. What does it mean to "file a claim?"

_____

_____

2. What will happen to your payment if the claim is not filled out correctly and completely?

_____

_____

Completing the claim form

Look at the claim form below. Remember, all the information on the form must be complete and accurate. The form has two parts. You fill out Part A. Your doctor may fill out Part B, which is not shown.

Line number 1 asks for your name and complete address, including your zip code.

Line number 2 asks for the Identification Number. When you sign up for health insurance through your employer, you are given an **identification card**. See the example on page 47. The card has an identification, or ID, number. This number identifies you as a member of the group health insurance plan. It also has other information such as telephone numbers you can call if you have questions.

---

*Keep a copy for your records.

National Association Insurance Company
555 Main Street
Anytown, USA 10101

PART A — EMPLOYEE MUST COMPLETE Failure to Answer All Questions May Delay Payment

Employee's Name	Street Address	City or Town	Zip Code
1.			

Identification Number	Social Security Number	Are You Still Employed? Yes ☐ No ☐	If No, Date Last Worked
2.			

Date of Birth	Maritial Status Single ☐ Divorced ☐ Married ☐ Widowed ☐	Name of Your Employer	Occupation
3.			

Spouse's Date of Birth	Spouse's Social Security No.	Is Your Spouse Employed Yes ☐ No ☐	If Yes, Name and Address of Spouse's Employer
4.			

Are You or Your Dependents Covered Under Another Group Insurance or Government Plan? 5. Yes ☐ No ☐	If Yes, Name and Address Policy Number / ID #		

Is Claim for a Dependent? Yes ☐ No ☐ 6.	If Yes, Dependent Name (first) (last)	Sex ☐ Male ☐ Female	Date of Birth	Relationship To Employee	If Dependent is a Child, Are You Entitled to a Tax Exemption? Yes ☐ No ☐

Is Claim for an Accident? 7. Yes ☐ No ☐	Date: Time:	Where Did It Occur?	While Working Yes ☐ No ☐	How Did It Occur?

SIGN HERE FOR ALL CLAIMS I hereby authorized any insurance co., hospital, or physician to release all information which may have a bearing on benefits payable under this plan of benefits. 8.	Date

PART B — DOCTOR OR SUPPLIER Doctor must complete OR attach itemized bill with diagnosis

National Association Insurance Company
Member ID Card

Edward Muniz
ID# 1 0521-6429

Call 1-800-555-1000

The next box on Line 2 asks for your social security number. The next two boxes should also be filled in.

Line 3 asks for your date of birth. It also asks for your **marital status**. If you are single, check that box. If you are married, check that box. Line 3 also asks for the name of your employer and your job, or occupation. Edward, for example, is a computer operator. He would put that information in the box titled "Occupation."

Line 4 should be filled out if you are married. Your spouse is your husband or wife. If you are single, you can leave this line blank.

Line 5 asks you if you or anyone in your family has other health insurance. Many families have more than one kind of insurance. If you do not have any other health insurance, check NO.

Line 6 asks if the health care is for a **dependent**. A dependent is someone, usually a child, you are responsible for. If the claim is for health care for your child, you will need to complete all the information in Line 6. If you do not have any dependents, check NO.

Line 7 asks if you were hurt in an accident. You need to fill in all the information in Line 7 if you check YES.

Line 8 asks you to sign the claim and include the date. If you do not sign the form, the insurance company will send it back to you. This will take time. This will also delay payment to you and your doctor.

When you have completed Part A, give the claim form to your doctor or attach a doctor's bill. Make sure you keep copies of everything you are sending to the insurance company. The company will send you a check if money is owed to you.

Reading an explanation of benefits statement

After the insurance company gets your claim, they review it. Then they will send you or your doctor a check. You also will get an **explanation of benefits statement**. This form will show each cost and how it was paid. It will show any deductible amounts and the copayment or coinsurance you owe. Look at the figure below to see how Edward's doctor visit was paid.

Name Edward Muniz ID# 5550-123	Explanation of Benefits Statement								Date 6/30/98
Description of Service	Date of Service From	Date of Service To	Charges	Reasonable & Customary Not covered	Reasonable & Customary Covered	Deductable applied	Coins.	%	Benefit paid
Office Visit	6/1/98	6/1/98	$75		$75	$75			$0
Blood Tests	6/1/98	6/1/98	$35		$35	$25	$10	80	$8
Antibiotic Shot	6/1/98	6/1/98	$25		$25	–	$25	80	$20
Vitamin C Pills	6/1/98	6/1/98	$12	$12					$0
Totals			$147	$12	$135	$100	$35		$28
						Actual Benefits Paid			$28
									Amount

Edward paid $147. This was his first visit and he had to pay his $100 deductible. He later got a check for $28 from the insurance company. The $12 cost of vitamin C pills was not covered. Edward's insurance benefit did not apply to $112 of the $147 doctor bill. The insurance company covered 80 percent of $35 coinsurance. The next time he visits the doctor, the insurance will cover more of the cost.

Lesson Review

Answer the following questions on the lines provided.

3. Why do you need to sign the completed claim form?

_____

_____

4. What do you do with the claim form after you have completed Part A, but before you send it to the insurance company?

_____

_____

5. What does the insurance company do when it receives the claim form?

_____

_____

6. What are two things that an explanation of benefits statement tells you?

_____

_____

Vocabulary Review

Write a definition for each vocabulary word on the lines provided.

7. doctor's bill

_____

_____

8. claim

_____

_____

9. dependent

_____

_____

10. identification card

_____

_____

11. file a claim

_____

_____

12. marital status

_____

_____

Portfolio

What Would You Say?

13. Work with a partner. Imagine your friend has just been to the doctor. Your friend has health insurance, but did not get a claim form for his insurance before he went to the doctor. Write a skit that explains to your friend why it is important to file a claim.

What Isn't Covered?

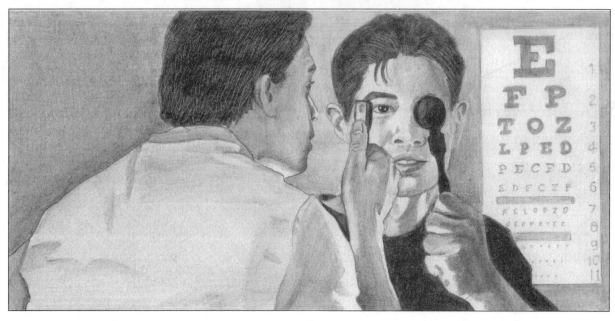

Most kinds of health insurance do not pay for eye exams.

Lesson Objectives

You will be able to

- identify services and items that might not be covered.
- explain how people can get other help paying for health care.

Words to Know

experimental health treatment	medicine or health care that is new and has not been tested
dental insurance	insurance similar to health insurance that pays for the basic costs of taking care of your teeth
Medicare	social security program to help pay for health care of disabled persons and senior citizens
Medicaid	government program to pay for the health care of people who cannot afford it
wellness plan	plan that helps pay for health care not covered by health insurance

Darren's job provided him with health insurance. He was very lucky. He was having trouble seeing and needed to go to an eye doctor. He went to see Marcia, the insurance person at his job.

"Hi, Marcia," said Darren. "I need to pick up a health insurance claim form."

"Hi, Darren," said Marcia. "Why do you need the claim form? Aren't you feeling well?"

"I'm feeling fine," said Darren. "But I'm having trouble with my eyes. I think I need glasses."

"But, Darren, our health insurance doesn't pay to see an eye doctor," said Marcia. "It doesn't pay for glasses either."

"I thought all our health care needs were paid for by the insurance," said Darren.

"Most things are," said Marcia, "but some are not."

Knowing What Your Health Insurance Pays For

Darren was surprised to find out his health insurance did not pay to see an eye doctor or for his glasses. Most kinds of health insurance do not pay for eye doctors. Darren wondered what else his health insurance did not pay for. He read the information about his plan. Darren was surprised at what he found.

Health insurance does not cover all of your health care costs. It covers your basic health care. It also pays for doctors, nurses, most medicines, stays in the hospitals, and any operations and tests you need.

Notice the word "need" in the last sentence. Your health insurance pays for the health care you need. It does not pay for many of the things you *want*.

You might be wondering what kinds of health care you might want instead of need. Some people don't like the shape of their noses. They would like to have a doctor change the shape. This is something a person wants, not needs. The cost is not covered by health insurance.

Most health insurance does not pay for the costs of vision and hearing tests. Most health insurance does not pay for hearing aids to help a person hear.

Many kinds of health insurance will not pay for **experimental health treatment**. An experimental health treatment is one that is new and has not been tested much. You might wonder what kind of health care is experimental. Doctors are often trying new medicines. They also often try new kinds of operations. These are examples of experimental treatment.

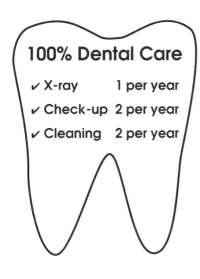

100% Dental Care

✔ X-ray   1 per year

✔ Check-up 2 per year

✔ Cleaning   2 per year

Most health insurance plans do not cover the costs of taking care of your teeth. You can, however, buy **dental insurance**. Dental insurance is similar to health insurance. It pays for all the basic costs of taking care of your teeth. It may also pay for part of major costs for tooth problems such as braces. Like health insurance, you have a premium and a yearly deductible for dental insurance.

Like Darren, you should read your health insurance plan carefully. Find out what kinds of health care are not covered.

Think About It

1. What is an experimental health treatment?

   _____

   _____

2. What cost do you have to pay if you have dental insurance?

   _____

Extra help to pay for your health care

Many companies offer health insurance to their employees. They may also offer help to pay for health care not covered by insurance. A **wellness plan** helps pay for health care not covered by health insurance. In many companies, the wellness plan pays a certain amount of money each year. Let's say that amount is $150. You can spend this money on any kind of health care not covered by your health insurance.

If your employer has a wellness plan, you will need to pay the doctor yourself. Then take the receipt for your health care to your employer. After you fill out a form, you will be paid back for your health care. If your health care costs more than the amount of your wellness plan, you have to pay that amount yourself.

Help from the government

Some people cannot afford health insurance or have very high medical bills. They can get help from some government plans. A person that is disabled, cannot work, or is a senior citizen can get coverage for health care from **Medicare**. People can apply for Medicare at the state social security office. People have to pay part of the cost of Medicare through copayments or some sort of insurance policy.

People whose incomes are below a certain level can get help for medical costs through **Medicaid**. People who are covered by Medicaid get health care that is paid by the government. People can apply for Medicaid at the state or county social services office.

Lesson Review

Answer the following questions on the lines provided.

3. What are three things that health insurance does not pay for?

_____

_____

_____

4. What is dental insurance? _____

_____

5. How does a wellness plan help pay for your health care costs?

_____

_____

Vocabulary Review

Write a definition for each vocabulary word on the lines provided.

6. experimental health treatment _____

_____

7. Medicare _____

_____

8. Medicaid _____

_____

Portfolio
What Would You Say?

9. Imagine you have just started a new job. One of your benefits is health insurance. But, you do not have a wellness plan. Write a letter to your new boss asking the company to offer a wellness plan. Give reasons why having a wellness plan is a valuable employee benefit.

UNIT REVIEW

Take Another Look

PART A — EMPLOYEE MUST COMPLETE		Failure to Answer All Questions May Delay Payment	
Employee's Name 1. Mark Peters	Street Address 1617 Schinder Road	City or Town Monroe	Zip Code 53566
Identification Number 2. 07513	Social Security No. 219-34-1716	Are You Still Employed? Yes ☑ No ☐	If No, Date Last Worked
Date of Birth 3. 9/21/65	Maritial Status Single ☐ Divorced ☐ Married ☑ Widowed ☐	Name of Your Employer Beliot Corporation	Occupation Supervisor
Spouse's Date of Birth 4. 5/8/63	Spouse's Social Security No.	Is Your Spouse Employed Yes ☑ No ☐	If Yes, Name and Address of Spouse's Employer Swiss Colony, Hwy 69, Monroe

Are You or Your Dependents Covered Under Another Group Insurance or Government Plan? 5. Yes ☐ No ☑	If Yes, Name and Address Policy Number / ID #

Is Claim for a Dependent? 6. Yes ☑ No ☐	If Yes, Dependent Name (first) Brock (last) Peters	Sex ☑ Male ☐ Female	Date of Birth 2/19/93	Relationship To Employee son	If Dependent is a Child, Are You Entitled to a Tax Exemption? Yes ☑ No ☐

Is Claim for an Accident? 7. Yes ☐ No ☑	Date: Time:	Where Did It Occur?	While Working Yes ☐ No ☐	How Did It Occur?

SIGN HERE FOR ALL CLAIMS   I hereby authorized any insurance co., hospital, or physician to release all information which may have a bearing on benefits payable under this plan of benefits.

8. _____   Date _____

Use the claim form above to answer the following questions.

1. Why is it important to fill out an insurance claim completely and accurately?

_____

_____

2. Who is the patient the claim is filed for?

_____

_____

3. What information is missing from this insurance claim?

_____

_____

4. What is the ID number for the member filing this claim?

_____

Reviewing What You Know

Answer the following on the lines provided.

5. What is the first thing you should do when looking for a primary care physician?

_____

_____

6. What is a medical emergency?

_____

_____

7. Explain how your health insurance pays for a medical emergency.

_____

_____

8. What are three kinds of health care your health insurance may not pay for?

_____

_____

Complete the following sentences.

9. You will get a(n) _____ from the insurance company that describes the kind of health care you received and how it was paid.

10. A(n) _____ is an accident or health problem for which you need help right away.

11. The part of the hospital that provides 24-hour care is the _____ _____.

12. A health treatment that is new and has not been tested is called _____ _____.

13. If you have _____ insurance, it will help pay for the basic costs of taking care of your teeth .

14. Some people can get help in paying for health care from two government programs called _____ and _____.

Cooperative Learning

15. Work with three classmates. Study several different health insurance plans. Make a poster that lists the types of care that are not covered by each kind of health insurance. Compare the lists for the different types of health insurance. Are they similar? What kinds of health care are covered by one health insurance plan and not another?

16. Work with a partner. Find out about dental insurance. You can get a copy of a dental insurance plan from your teacher. Find out what the monthly premium and yearly deductible are for the dental insurance.

GLOSSARY

affordable (uh-FORD-uh-buhl) *adj.* low enough in cost to pay for without difficulty   4

allergic, allergy (uh-LUR-jihk) *adj.* having a bad reaction such as a rash, upset stomach, itchy watery eyes and nose, or trouble breathing; usually caused by something you eat, touch, or breathe   16

claim (klaym) *n.* form that must be completed by you and the doctor for the insurance company; it describes the kind of health care you received   45

COBRA (KOH-bruh) *n.* plan that allows you to continue your health insurance for a certain amount of time if you lose your job   10

coinsurance (KOH-ihn-SHOOR-uhns) *n.* amount of your health care costs you pay after the insurance company pays, not including the deductible   23

copayment (KOH-pay-muhnt) *n.* fixed dollar amount you pay for a specific health care service, such as a visit to a doctor's office 23

coverage (KUV-uhr-ihj) *n.* types of health care insurance will pay for   4

dental insurance (DEHN-tuhl ihn-SHOOR-uhns) *n.* insurance similar to health insurance that pays for the basic costs of taking care of your teeth   52

dependent (dee-PEHN-duhnt) *n.* someone, usually a child, that an adult is responsible for   47

doctor's bill (DAHK-tuhrs bihl) *n.* a list from the doctor showing what was wrong with you, what was done, and how much it cost   45

emergency (ee-MER-juhn-see) *n.* accident or health problem for which you need help right away   41

emergency room (ee-MER-juhn-see room) *n.* part of a hospital that provides 24-hour emergency care   41

employee benefit (ehm-PLOI-ee BEHN-uh-fiht) *n.* something an employer provides, such as paid vacation or health insurance, in addition to your salary   9

employer (ehm-PLOI-uhr) *n.* person or company for which you work   9

experimental health treatment (ehk-SPAIR-uh-muhnt-uhl hehlth TREET-muhnt) *n.* medicine or health care that is new and has not been tested   51

explanation of benefits statement (ehks-pluh-NAY-shuhn uv BEHN-uh-fihts STAYT-muhnt) *n.* a form that the insurance company sends to you to show how your health care costs are being paid   48

file a claim (FEYE-uhl uh klaym) *vt.* to fill out a claim form completely and correctly, then send the form and the doctor's bills to your insurance company   45

group insurance plan (groop ihn-SHOOR-uhns plan) *n.* plan purchased by a group that covers many people and lowers the cost of health insurance   9

health insurance (hehlth ihn-SHOOR-uhns) *n.* kind of insurance that pays for part of your medical expenses and health care   3

HMO (Health Maintenance Organization) (hehlth MAY-tuhn-uhns OR-guh-neye-ZAY-shuhn) *n.* health insurance plan in which your health care needs are covered through a network only   28

identification card (eye-DEHN-tuh-fih-KAY-shuhn kard) *n.* card you get from your employer that identifies you as a member of the group health insurance plan   46

individual insurance plan (IHN-duh-VIHJ-oo-uhl ihn-SHOOR-uhns plan) *n.* plan purchased by an individual for one person and his or her family   11

in-network (ihn-neht-werk) *adj.* going to doctors, nurses, or hospitals that are part of a network   28

injury (IN-juh-ree) *n.* harm or damage to a person   5

insurance (ihn-SHOOR-uhns) *n.* protection you buy from a company to help you pay the costs of health care or damage from fire or accidents   3

Managed Care Plan (MAN-ihjed kair plan) *n.* kind of health insurance in which you may choose the doctor or you may use a network; helps control the cost of health care   29

marital status (MAR-uh-tuhl STAT-uhs) *n.* tells whether you are single or married   47

medical history (MEHD-ihk-uhl HIHST-uh-ree) *n.* record of your health from the time you were born to the present   15

Medicaid (MEHD-ih-kayd) *n.* government program to pay for the health care of people who cannot afford it   53

Medicare (MEHD-ih-kair) *n.* social security program to help pay for health care of disabled persons and senior citizens   52

network (NEHT-werk) *n.* group of doctors and hospitals that provide health care at a reduced cost to its members   28

options (AHP-shuhns) *n.* things that can be chosen   33

out-of-network (owt-uv-neht-werk) *adj.* going to doctors, nurses, or hospitals that are not part of a network   29

out-of-pocket limit (owt-uv-PAH-kiht LIHM-iht) *n.* greatest amount of money you pay for health care in one year; point at which insurance pays 100 percent   24

precertification (pree-SER-tih-fih-KAY-shuhn) *n.* approval from a person's health insurance for a hospital visit; must be approved before the person goes to the hospital   41

pre-existing condition (PREE-ehg-zihst-ing KUHN-dihsh-uhn) *n.* health problem a person has before he or she buys health insurance; may delay the start of insurance coverage   12

premium (PREE-mee-uhm) *n.* the amount of money you pay each month to have health insurance   21

preventive care (pree-VEHNT-ihv kair) *n.* seeing a doctor while you are healthy to prevent becoming sick   29

primary care physician (PREYE-mair-ee kair fih-ZIHSH-uhn) *n.* doctor you select from a network; doctor you see for most of your health care needs   39

reasonable and customary costs (REE-zuhn-uh-buhl and KUHS-tuhm-AIR-ee kosts) *n.* standard charges for health care in a geographic area; costs above this are not covered by insurance   24

social security number (SOH-shuhl sih-KYOOR-uh-tee NUHM-buhr) *n.* identification number given to a person by the United States government   15

Traditional Care Plan (truh-DIHSH-uhn-uhl kair plan) *n.* kind of health insurance in which you choose the doctors you see   27

vaccination (VAK-suh-NAY-shuhn) n. shot to protect you from getting a certain disease   16

waiting period (WAYT-ing PIHR-ee-uhd) *n.* time between when you start a job and when your insurance coverage begins   11

wellness plan (WEHL-nuhs plan) *n.* plan that helps pay for health care not covered by health insurance   52

yearly deductible (YIHR-lee dee-DUKT-uh-buhl) *n.* the amount you must spend each year before the insurance company pays anything   22

RESOURCES

Here is some information about typical health insurance plans.
The following charts show the kinds of health care covered by
a Traditional Care Plan, a Managed Care Plan, a Health
Maintenance Organization, and a Dental Care Plan.

Traditional Care Plan

This plan includes a yearly deductible of $200 per individual,
$400 per family. The plan covers health care costs described
below after the yearly deductible is paid by the insured
individual or family.

Type of Care	Costs Covered by Plan	Costs You Pay
Doctor's Office Visit	80% of cost	20% of cost
Preventive Care	80% of cost up to $300 limit per year	20% of cost under the $300 yearly limit; 100% of cost above $300 per year
Hospital Stay	80% of cost	20% of cost
Surgical Care	80% of cost	20% of cost
Emergency Care	80% of cost	20% of cost
Prescription Medicines	80% of cost	20% of cost
Mental Health and Substance Abuse Treatment: Outside a Hospital	50% of cost up to $2,000 limit per year	50% of cost under the $2,000 yearly limit; 100% of cost above $2,000 per year
Mental Health and Substance Abuse Treatment: In a Hospital	80% of cost for 30 days	20% of cost for 30 days
Other costs such as X-rays and lab tests	80% of cost	20% of cost
Hearing and vision exams	not covered	100%
Hearing aids, eyeglasses, and contact lenses	not covered	100%

Note that this plan pays for 100% of covered health care costs
after you pay a yearly out-of-pocket limit. The out-of-pocket limit
is $2,000 for an individual, $4,000 for a family.

Managed Care Plan

There is no yearly deductible when the insured individual or family uses in-network doctors and hospitals. The insured individual or family may go out-of-network and still be covered. These costs are paid only after a yearly deductible of $200 per individual or $400 per family.

Type of Care	Costs Covered In-Network	Costs Covered Out-of-Network	Costs You Pay
Doctor's Office Visit	100% after $15 copayment for each visit	70% of cost	$15 per visit in-network; 30% of cost out-of-network
Preventive Care	100% after $15 copayment	70% of cost up to $300 per year	$15 per visit in-network; 30% of cost up to $300 per year
Hospital Stay	90% of cost	70% of cost	10% in-network; 30% out-of-network
Surgical Care	90% of cost	70% of cost	10% in-network; 30% out-of-network
Emergency Care	100% after $25 copayment	100% after $25 copayment	$25 copayment
Prescription Medicines	100% of cost after $10 copayment for each prescription	70% of cost	$10 copayment in-network; 30% out-of-network
Mental Health and Substance Abuse Treatment: Outside a Hospital	100% of cost after $10 copayment up to $2,000 per year	50% of cost up to $2,000 limit per year	$10 copayment in-network; 50% out-of-network; up to $2,000 yearly limit
Mental Health and Substance Abuse Treatment: In a Hospital	90% up to 30 days	70% up to 30 days	10% in-network; 30% out-of-network
Other costs such as X-rays and lab tests	100% after $15 copayment	70% of cost	$15 copayment in-network; 30% out-of-network
Hearing and vision exams	100% after $15 copayment	70% of cost	$15 copayment in-network; 30% out-of-network
Hearing aids, eyeglasses and contact lenses	not covered	not covered	100% of cost

Note that this plan pays for 100% of covered health care costs after you pay a yearly out-of-pocket limit. The out-of-pocket limit is $1,000 for an individual, $2,000 for a family.

Health Maintenance Organization (HMO)

This plan gives 100 percent coverage for most medical costs. There is no deductible to pay before you are covered. There are copayments for some kinds of care. You must use the HMO's network of doctors and hospitals to be covered. The HMO does not pay for treatment by out-of-network doctors or hospitals, except for emergencies.

Type of Care	Costs Covered by Plan	Costs You Pay
Doctor's Office Visit	100% of cost	$10 copayment for each visit
Preventive Care	100% of cost	nothing
Hospital Stay	100% of cost	nothing
Surgical Care	100% of cost	nothing
Emergency Care	100% of cost	$25 copayment for each emergency
Prescription Medicines	100% of cost	$10 copayment for each prescription
Mental Health Treatment: Outside a Hospital	50% of cost for 30 visits per year	50% of cost for 30 visits per year
Mental Health Treatment: Inside a Hospital	100% of cost up to 30 days per year	all costs after 30 days per year
Other medical costs: lab tests, X-rays	100% of cost	nothing
Hearing and vision exams	100% of cost	nothing
Hearing aids, eyeglasses, and contact lenses	not covered	100% of cost

Dental Health Plan

This plan includes a yearly deductible of $50 for an individual, or $100 for a family. The plan covers dental care costs shown below after the yearly deductible is paid by the insured individual or family.

Type of Care	Costs Covered by Plan	Costs You Pay
Preventive Care: exams, X-rays, teeth cleaning	100% of cost	nothing
Basic Care: filling cavities, tooth extraction, oral surgery	80% of cost	20% of cost
Major Care: bridges, dentures	50% of cost	50% of cost
Orthodontic Care: braces, retainers	50% of cost up to $1,000 per person lifetime limit	50% of cost up to $1,000 per person lifetime limit; 100% of cost after $1,000